Dream Dogz

Freedom

Remote Collar Training

Victoria Warfel

Richard Warfel

For information contact:
Dream Dogz, LLC
Gainesville, Florida
www.DreamK9.com

(352) 278-7404
DreamK9@iCloud.com

Updated: August 2015
The dog in the photos is Arrow, our Belgian Shepherd Malinois.

Preface

I started off as a food-based "clicker trainer," and was convinced that I would never use one those "torture devices" otherwise known as "shock collars." Then I had a session with a new client and her two dogs that changed my dog training path.

The dogs were out of control crazy on walks, barking and lunging at everyone and everything. It was going to take quite some time to work with them, first separately, under threshold, gradually upping distractions, then working both of them together. After I explained this to the owner, she told me that before she moved to town, she had a session with a trainer who used a remote training collar with her dogs. I was up front with her, and told her that I have never used one before, did not know much about them, other than what I had been told, and would like to feel it for myself. You see, for all that I was against them, I had never felt one or seen one used appropriately. And guess what, the people who *were* using them effectively weren't coming to me for training - they didn't need me! So she put the receiver in my hand, and went to push the button - and I dropped the receiver like it was a hot potato... but she hadn't touched anything. I thought it would hurt, and that is what I was expecting and had prepared myself for. A painful feeling, a taser. I picked the receiver up again, and held it while she pressed the button. And guess what? It didn't hurt. I barely felt anything. The sensation was like a TENS unit at the doctor. I asked her for two weeks so I could learn the proper way to use the collar and incorporate into our training.

This was years ago, and it was hard to find any information online. This is why, today, we make sure we put out a lot of information on YouTube, Facebook, Instagram, our website and our blog. I talked with some of the best trainers who were using the remote collars, and we came up with a game plan. I was excited to try this new tool for myself, and picked up a remote training collar from one of the local pet stores to try it out. It was terrible! I found out there is a big difference between a "cheap" remote collar and a good remote collar. For that reason, we will only use good remote collars, our preferred brand is from E-Collar Technologies. I returned the pet store collar and ordered a good collar online. When it came in, I first used it with Jedi, my German Shepherd, and was amazed at how quickly she responded. Then, I borrow dogs from my friends and incorporated it into their training, and we were very happy with the results.

After the couple weeks of learning and experimenting, I had the second session with the two dogs whose owner had introduced me to the remote collar. A week or so later, she could walk her dogs, together, without any problems. Her goal was taking her formerly reactive and aggressive dogs to a dog park. Within the month, we had them at one of the local dog parks and also in a dog daycare. These results happened in only 1 month! By incorporating the remote collar into our training, we saw results in weeks that would have taken months and maybe years.

For the next couple years, I continued experimenting with the remote collar. For dogs who were not getting the "regular" training we were doing, I would approach the owners with the idea of trying the remote collar with their dog. I was getting fantastic results with all different types of dogs and all different behavior issues.

When I came out as a balanced trainer who uses a remote collar as one of the tools in my toolbox, I received backlash from a couple of people in the community. However, these huge changes I was making in my client's lives - and the hope I was giving to people who thought their dog was beyond help - were worth the few negative comments, which were from people I had never even met.

Freedom was actually started before Dogmanship, it was my first experience with the effectiveness that is the foundation of Dogmanship, the pressure (button on) and release (button off). For more information on this type of training, check out another of our books - Dogmanship - which goes into detail on those methods.

-Victoria

1. Introduction

We are remote collar training specialists, and Freedom is our very own training method. We use Freedom for behavior modification, for obedience training, and any training where a leash is not practical.

Your dog will have **Freedom**. Not just off-leash Freedom, but Freedom to be part of your family.

We use Freedom to rehabilitate dogs that are aggressive, reactive, shy, bold, young, old, big, little, nervous, fearful, rambunctious and everything in between. We have found that the nervous, shy, fearful dogs do very well, because the dog gains confidence from the clear communication that you will learn to provide with the remote collar.

Freedom will build your dog's pack drive, teaching your dog to focus on you and ignore distractions. It will also help your dog to be in the right state of mind, and once that happens, many behavior issues will disappear.

2. Freedom Guidelines

We have some guidelines to help you start Freedom and get the most out of this training with your dog.

• Your dog has to be able to walk by and ignore dogs, people, and other distractions. Playtime is great! However, not every dog you meet will be a playmate for your dog, and your dog does not need to say hello to everyone and everything.

• At Dream Dogz Behavior Center, dogs in training DO NOT GREET. We do not permit butt sniffing or nose touching between dogs. Dogs are here for a number of reasons, including aggression rehabilitation. We set all dogs up for success. We give all dogs and people the space they need. We will show you how to do a proper introduction between dogs when the time is right. When you are walking with your dog, do not allow people or other dogs to greet your dog. Simply tell them that your dog is in training and continue on your way. Check our youtube.com/dreamdogz video - Advocate for your Dog.

• Watch your dog. Do not get distracted and let your dog wander to the end of the leash while you are talking to someone. We do not want your dog getting into mischief or getting too close to other dogs or people.

• Practice. Your e-collar is a fantastic training tool, but it is not a magic wand. You have to do the training to see results. The more you practice at home, the better your dog will do, and the more comfortable you will be with your new training tool. Some dogs get it right away, while others need a few sessions before it starts to click. Limit training sessions to 10-15 minutes and give your dog time afterwards to absorb the new knowledge. We usually crate the dog for this "soak time."

• Be consistent in your words, voice, and motion. Follow through with what you ask for.

• Repetition is key. Train each step dozens of times, increasing distance, distraction, and duration as needed. While it is important to encourage your dog to increase their abilities, it is also often necessary to take a step back to the next easiest when the new behavior seems too difficult at the moment. A few minutes later, you will find it much easier, so will your dog.

• Freedom is a very clear way to communicate with your dog. Everything is Pressure On (Stim) and Pressure Off (no

Stim). This pairs nicely with our Dogmanship style of training. Dogs benefit the most when we start with the prong collar or slip lead until your dog understands the concept of pressure & release. Once they understand it, we can easily transfer the leash pressure & release to the remote training collar pressure & release. However, we have started many dogs with the remote training collar, but we prefer to give our clients plenty of tools to use with their dog.

• **Stim, Turn & Walk Away.** Otherwise known as *The Warfel Way*. This is key. If you do not know what to do, you can not go wrong if you Stim Turn & Walk Away with your leashed dog. Stim Turn & Walk Away is described in detail later in this book.

3. Freedom Advantages

We think every dog should be Freedom trained. There will come a time where your dog is off leash, someone may have left the gate open, or perhaps you accidentally dropped the leash. No matter the reason, communication with your dog at a distance and off leash is essential. There are many advantages to remote collar training, here are a few.

Remote collar training provides precise timing at the push, and release, of a button. You will instantly be able to communicate with your dog at a distance of up to one mile away with some collars. The collars that we typically use have a half-mile range, which is more than enough for most dogs. Your voice cannot carry this distance, but the signal from the remote to the collar will.

Did we mention the ease of operation? All you need to do is push a button, no matter how large and strong, or small and dainty, your dog is. The remote training collar is the great equalizer, and the training level can be set to just what your dog needs at that time. As an added bonus, the remote training collar is a neutral communicator. You are not the source of the correction or consequence. Well, you are, but your dog will not see it that way. For example, if your dog is a counter surfer, stealing food from the kitchen countertops, you do not want your dog to leave that alone *only* when you are around. Countertops are off limits. Period.

For dogs who may not like people, Freedom offers the ability to train the dog hands-off. We see amazing results time and again using our Freedom method in the rehabilitation of reactive and aggressive dogs, as well as shy and fearful dogs.

4. Freedom Requirements

Remember when I told you about my first experience with a remote training collar? Do not be cheap when purchasing one of these, you will regret it. Instead, buy a good quality collar and you will be able to train many dogs on it. In our experience, the three best brands are E-Collar Technologies, Dogtra, and Tritronics/Garmin. Our favorite brand, and the one we highly recommend, is E-Collar Technologies (ecollar.com). We always have them on hand. The quality, warranty, customer service, features, and - of course - product, are excellent.

E-Collar Technologies remote training collars are reliable, rechargeable, and waterproof. They provide a consistent level of stimulation that is a requirement for our Freedom method. Since they have 100+ levels of stimulation (stim), we can find the lowest level that your dog responds to.

Most dogs do very well on the Easy Educator EZ-900 and the Mini Educator ET-300. We describe how the buttons work, how to program the collars, the differences between the collars, and more, on our YouTube channel (youtube.com/dreamdogz).

The equipment must be used properly. Here are four steps for successful training. The collar must be:

1. Charged. All models allow you to charge both receiver and transmitter at the same time. Be sure that your equipment is fully charged, it only takes a few hours.

2. Turned on. Both pieces must be turned on prior to use. It is easy to forget, so double check instead of being frustrated later.

3. Snug enough. Both contact points have to reach your dog's skin thru their fur. Make sure your contact points are the correct length, and make sure the collar is fit properly. You may be used to your flat collar being very loose on your dog. That is fine, but your remote collar is not the same. If the remote collar is loose, it is not effective. Our advice is "If you think it is too tight, it is probably just right." Keep in mind that when you are putting something around a dog's neck, it is common for your dog to flex their neck muscles making their neck two or three notches bigger. So a few minutes later when they relax their neck, the collar is loose. Double check to make sure you have the correct fit. If your receiver is loose, it will slide around and lose contact. So if your dog shakes and the receiver

slides around, it is too loose.

Once the collar is fit correctly, you may want to trim the extra strap, remember to measure twice and cut once.

E-Collar Technologies has three alternative collar straps that make fitting your dog easier. With the quick-snap collar, you don't have to find the right hole that your dog uses, instead, after it is initially fit, you just snap it on and off. The bungee collar allows the collar some give. The quick-snap/bungee combination collar gives you both of those features, it provides the best collar fit possible for your dog, and is the collar strap what we use with our own dogs.

4. Position. For optimum performance, we have found that the position of the receiver plays an important role. For most dogs, you will want the receiver high on your dog's neck, usually above the other collars your dog is wearing. In addition, most dogs respond best when the receiver is positioned behind an ear or by their cheek. Avoid positioning it near the throat.

We have a few more words of advice when fitting your remote training collar. If your dog is not responding, try a different position on your dog's neck. If your dog has a long coat, wiggle the receiver to make sure the contact points reach through the coat. You can change the contact points if your dog has a longer or thick coat, or you can shave a patch on your dog's neck for the collar. If you have a small dog, like a shih tzu or a yorkie, we suggest changing to the comfort adapter for the small collar receiver. E-Collar Technologies has these available for both short hair and long hair coats. The comfort adapter also works well for dogs that wear the collar longer than 8 hours each day. If your dog wears the e-collar for longer than 2 hours at a time, loosen it, move it, and re-fasten it.

If your dog is not responding, make sure the above requirements have been met. You should also turn the receiver (your dog's collar) and transmitter (your part) off, and turn them on again.

In addition to the remote training collar requirements, your dog will be wearing additional equipment when starting training. Your dog must wear another collar. You may want to start with your secondary collar as a prong collar or slip collar, then you have the option of transitioning to a flat collar, so all of the communication comes from the remote training collar.

You will use a 6' flat leash attached to the secondary collar. Never attach a leash to your remote training collar. If you attach a leash to that, you will move it and the contact will be unreliable. You will also use a 15' to 20' long flat leash.

You may use treats or a favorite toy to reward your dog. However, most of the time we mark desired behavior with "Good," along with praise, pets, and a smile on our face.

For the transmitter (your part), we attach a key ring to the ring provided. Then we clip the lanyard onto the key ring, and also add a carabiner so we can clip the remote onto a belt loop, set of keys, purse strap, or whatever we are using. E-Collar Technologies has a variety of options, including the lanyard that comes with the collar, but this is what we prefer. You can use any of the accessories with this set up.

For the receiver (your dog's collar), we add a Boomerang Tags CollarTag beside the transmitter on the collar strap. This identification tag is silent and does not jingle. If you have multiple dogs, it helps to identify whose collar is whose.

5. Frequently Asked Questions

How long will my dog wear the e-collar?

Your dog will wear the e-collar when you are spending time with your dog, when you are training or walking your dog, when your dog is outside with you, or when you think you are going to need it. Your collar does you no good if it is on the shelf when you need it. Our philosophy is: it is better to be prepared and not need it, instead of needing it and not having it.

The collar should be off your dog when your dog is crated, your dog is sleeping, you are sleeping, or you leave the house without your dog.

Remember to set your dog up for success. **Your dog should be leashed and e-collared, as noted above, for the first 14-21 days, minimum.** This enables you to guide your dog as needed.

Remember, if your dog wears the e-collar for longer than 2 hours at a time, loosen it, move it, and re-fasten it.

How long do I practice?

We use low level Stim and take it slow. Some dogs start to get it during their very first training session. For other dogs, it takes two, three or four sessions before they understand the concept. During personal training sessions at Dream Dogz, these are going to be homework sessions with you, not training sessions with us. During Board & Train packages, your dog will return home fluent on the remote training collar.

The first session gets your dog used to the small tickle on their neck. The more you practice - aim for **10-15 minutes a few times each day** - the better your dog will understand what the Stim means and the quicker your dog will learn. Remember to crate your dog afterwards so your dog can soak in what you just taught.

Should I start with Momentary or Constant stim?

We start dogs with Constant. The Momentary is just too quick to communicate effectively with most dogs in the beginning. As your dog understands what the collar means, you may be able to use Momentary to stop undesired behaviors before they escalate. Think of the stim as your cell phone signal. Would you rather have a clear conversation or would you rather hear every other or third word said? With Constant, your dog will "hear" everything you "say."

While on Constant, the Stim only lasts as long as you hold the button, with an automatic shut off if you hold the button for longer than 10 seconds (on most units). While on Momentary, the Stim only lasts a moment, no matter how long you hold the button.

We refer to the Momentary & Constant buttons as Stim, for stimulation. When we say to press the Stim button, for most dogs, that means press the Constant button.

Can I just use Vibrate?

Some people may want to use only Vibrate on their dog. A word of warning, Vibrate cannot be controlled and some dogs overreact. With most collars, you cannot select a Vibrate level. It is simply Vibrate. However, with Stim you precisely control the level of intensity that you are using with your dog.

The Vibrate lasts as long as you hold the button, with an automatic shut off if you hold the button for longer than 10 seconds (on most units). We sometimes recommend Vibrate when your dog is stuck on a scent, or focused on a squirrel, and ignoring you.

Many owners of deaf dogs want to only use Vibrate. This is a disservice to the dog, and handicaps them because of human emotions. We use the Stim on shy dogs, fearful dogs, and even deaf dogs.

The Easy Educator EZ-900 offers you the ability to download software and adjust the button settings on your computer. This will give you multiple Vibrate options.

What training level should I use?

When your dog listens to you!

On the E-Collar Technology models that we recommended earlier, Easy Educator EZ-900 and Mini Educator ET-300, we have found that many dogs start between levels 3-8. When we begin a dog on Freedom, we make sure the collar is fit properly, then we start at a level 1, 2, or 3, and see how the dog responds. If the dog responds well, that is the level we work the dog. If, after a few minutes of training, the dog ignores us, we turn the collar up a level. If the dog twitches, jumps, or flinches, we turn the collar down a level or few. **Remember, the goal is not to *force* the dog to listen by turning the level up, but to *encourage* the dog to listen by turning the level down. And if the Stim is helpful, the dog will try very hard to notice it.**

Think of Goldilocks. The level can be *too low, too high, or just right*. When there are more distractions, you may need to dial up the number. When there are fewer distractions, you may be able to dial down the number. Do not get hung up on the number, just remember that it is should be "just right" for the situation, not too low or too high.

If you see your dog:

- looking at you

- listening to you

- following you

- paying attention to you

    ...then you are on the right level.

If you see your dog:

- ear twitching

- head shaking

- jumping up

- squeaking

    ...then turn down a level or two.

If you see your dog:

- ignoring you

    ...then turn up a level or two.

Remember, this is a fluid training level and will change based on the environment and situation.

There are three levels you will be using:

Intro level - Allows you and your dog to learn about the collar, how it works, and how to turn it off. As stated above, this may be between levels 3-8.

Work level - As your dog understands what the collar means, you may have to occasionally dial up a little higher. For some dogs, this may be between levels 5-15.

Proof level - As your dog totally understands the training, and tests the limits, remember the collar needs to be just right for the situation. You do not want to push the button continuously. For some dogs, this may be between levels 8-20+.

The numbers we listed here are only a guide. Each dog is an individual and what works with one may not be effective on the next. However, if we are working your dog at a level 4, and you go home, you should be around there. If you are getting up to a level 10 or higher, and not seeing any response, check your equipment and what you are asking your dog to do. You should also try changing out your contact points to get a better connection with your dog. We have had dogs start at a level 1, and we have had dogs start at a level 20+.

How do I train my dog to be off-leash?

Your leash may disappear in a few weeks. During your first weeks of training, your dog should be leashed when wearing the e-collar so you can guide with the leash as needed. You do not want your dog confused about what the collar means or what to do about it.

When your dog is doing well on your 6' leash, switch to your 15' leash. Hold the end of the long leash while working your dog. As your dog is doing well, and does not get to the end of your long leash, you can drop the leash, but be ready to step on it if needed. As your dog does well on a dropped dragging leash, try off-leash (in a safe, fenced area).

It looks like this -

1. guide with your 6' leash and Stim. When you do not need to guide...

2. hold the end of your 15' leash. When it stays loose...

3. drop the 15' leash. Be ready to step on it...

4. take your dog off-leash, in a fenced area to start with.

For some dogs, the collar may disappear in a few months. When you start, you are pushing the button. A lot. As the days go by, your dog will understand and listen to you, and you will not need to push the button as much. There will come times when you need to dial up. Remember, we need the right level for your dog. If your dog is not listening to you, increase your dog's motivation by dialing up the level. **Because dogs are living beings, we recommend any time your dog is off-leash, your dog is on-remote training collar.**

But when can my dog stop wearing the collar?

I have insurance on my vehicle, and I always wear a seatbelt. I hope I never *have* to use either of them, but I have them *just in case*. The same thing holds true for your e-collar. When you take your dog off-leash, think of the collar as a safety back up. If your dog is off-leash, your dog is on your remote training collar. Your e-collar is one of the more expensive training tools you may purchase for your dog, so use it. It does you no good if it is at home when you and your dog are hiking in the woods together.

For the first week or so of Freedom training, we want you and your dog to be fully comfortable with the collar and how to use it. So you will push the button a lot, it may be for a quick tap, or a longer time. You will learn how to read your dog, and practice dialing up and down. If your dog responds too quick, before you can push the button, we want you to think "Awww. I didn't get to push the button."

What does the collar feel like?

Before we start training your dog, we will find YOUR training level. Hold the receiver on your arm, your leg, or on the palm of your hand, make sure both contact points are touching you. Press the Vibrate button. Did you feel that?

Start at number 1 and press the Stim button two or three times. If you feel that, you have found your working level. If you did not feel that, dial up a number and repeat until you do notice the stim. I think you will be surprised at your level, and how much it feels like a TENS unit.

6. FREEDOM TRAINING

Commands We Use

"Sit" - sit on the ground until released

"Down" - lay your body, with elbows touching the ground, until released

"Off" - get off something, such as the couch (do not use "Down" for this one)

"Come" or "Here" - come here to me

"Place" - go to this object and stay within its boundaries until released

"Let's Go" - let us go on a walk together.

"Free" or "Break" - you are free to do what you would like, within reason

"Good" - that is what I want you to do, good job

"No" or "Nope" - go back to what you were doing

"Stay" - not a command we use. Sit, Down, and Place have implied Stay, until released. So remember to release with "Let's Go" or "Free."

With Freedom, we often layer the e-collar over the commands. How we do this is when we give the command to the dog, we push the button and guide the dog into position. When the dog is in the correct position, we release the button and praise the dog "Good," to mark that position.

You say:

Command ("Sit") ----------------------------> Praise ("Good")

You do:

Press button ------------------------------------> Release button

Your dog does:

Dog standing ----(Guide dog into position)----> Dog sits

Check out our YouTube Channel - www.YouTube.com/DreamDogz.

You can watch our Freedom playlist or search "Freedom" for videos on the training shown in this book.

Enjoy!

Motivation Level

Do not think of the Stim as a negative. Freedom uses low level stim as a means to communicate helpful information to your dog. It is not a punisher. If your dog needs more motivation, dial up a level.

Follow Me / Come

This is the first thing we train with the e-collar, one of the benefits is this increases your dog's pack drive/social drive. Once your dog will Follow you, "Come" naturally follows. You will also start *The Warfel Way* (**Stim Turn and Walk Away**), which solves many behavior issues

(described in detail later in this book).

Phase 1. We want you to feel comfortable using the remote collar while you find the level that your dog first notices the stim.

Your dog will be wearing the e-collar (begin at level 1) & a secondary collar with leash attached. Walk straight ahead with your dog. Do not command your dog to "Heel," just walk. Your dog will likely walk or run past you. Before your dog gets to the end of the leash, Stim Turn and Walk Away (*The Warfel Way*).

- STIM/Pressure On - press the button until your dog looks at you, guiding your dog towards you as with gentle leash pressure as you turn 180 degrees away from your dog and walk away.

- STOP STIM/Pressure Off and praise - stop pressing the button when your dog pays attention and moves toward you. You can mark this behavior with a "Good."

Repeat this a few times, looking for any body language that your dog has noticed the stim. If your dog did not notice the stim and required leash guidance to follow you, then turn the stim up one level, and repeat.

It is very likely that your dog will feel the stim without showing any reaction. Carefully observe if your dog is reacting to the stim more than the leash. If you cannot see or feel any reaction to the stim, do not continue past level 10. At level 10, assume that your dog feels it and repeat a few more times, turning and guiding with the leash so your dog will follow you.

As you feel comfortable with the e-collar, and your dog is responding, it is time to move on to the next step. Do not worry if your dog does not respond without leash guidance, they are just learning that the tiny sensation has meaning.

Phase 2. Starting from level 1 again, walk with your leashed dog. Stop your forward movement and let your dog go ahead of you. Before the leash gets tight, Stim.

- If your dog turns and comes to you, you are working at the right level.

- If your dog does not turn and come to you, dial up a number and try again. If your dog does not respond after 6 or more turns, dial the level up one number and repeat. Remember the level is fluid, we do not want you to be stuck on a number, but we want you to lower and raise the number as needed, so you are working on the lowest level that your dog responds to. With the E-Collar Technology collars we recommend, most dogs start between 3-8. If your dog is getting to level 8-10 without responding, turn the level to 5 and work your dog for a couple more training sessions in a less distracting environment. Some dogs take longer to "get it." You do not want to work too high, too soon.

Phase 3. The next step is to add Come. As your dog is coming when you press the Stim, call "Come" or "Here," as you back up. Try to be behind your dog so your dog does not see you before you call your dog. If your dog has a history of ignoring you when you call "Come," then switch to "Here," as it will be a new command with which you will train your dog.

We do not train Come from a stationary (stay) command. We train a distracted Come, which is what happens in real life. Your dog is distracted by all the smells, sights, and squirrels in the environment. When you call your dog to "Come!", you want your dog to spin around and race back to you at top speed.

Set your dog up for success. Remember to always **guide your dog with gentle leash pressure**, as needed, when introducing a new command. Work your dog on the 15′ long leash, holding just the end of it so your dog has the feel of distance and freedom.

Phase 4. When your dog is doing well and does not need leash guidance, drop the long leash and repeat, in a fenced area. Be ready to step on the leash if needed.

Phase 5. When your dog is doing well and you do not need to step on the leash, take your dog off-leash and repeat, in a fenced area.

You say:

"Come" -------------------------------->"Good"

You do:

Press button -------------------------> Release button

Your dog does:

Dog ----(Guide dog into position)------> Dog turns head to you

Heel

Take your dog on structured walks twice each day, for 15 minutes each, minimum. Your dog must walk at your side and at your pace. Dogs are predators, with eyes in front of their head, so they can see what is in front of them. Your legs will be a visual marker for where your dog should position their body during your walks together.

If you only ask for a loose leash while walking, your dog will not know if they are one foot in front of you or six feet in front of you, until they feel the consequence. Make life easy for your dog, require your dog to walk at your side and at your pace. This is teamwork training, and provides physical *and* mental exercise for your dog, leading to a happy, tired, calm dog.

When you are out walking your dog, your dog does not have to greet other dogs or people. If you meet someone on your walk who would like to say hello, tell them that your dog is in training and continue on your way. It is your responsibility to advocate for your dog, and keep your dog safe. This includes greeting people and dogs that your dog is comfortable with. If your dog does not feel comfortable with people, your dog does not greet people. If your dog does not feel comfortable with other dogs, your dog does not greet other dogs, no butt-sniffing, no nose-touching, no staring. Do not permit your dog to bite the leash or sniff the ground during walks. However, you can give your dog "sniff breaks" as a reward for good behavior, but they will be on your terms.

Phase 1. With your dog on your left side, or your right side, tell your dog "Let's go."

• Start walking with your dog, if dog's hind legs are at your hip or ahead of you, Stim.

• STOP Stim & praise when your dog's front legs are at your hip or behind you.

Your dog must stay on whatever side you start your dog on. If your dog starts on your left side, your dog must stay on your left side. If your dog tries to switch sides, Stim and guide your dog back into position. You do not want your dog circling you or tripping you.

Phase 2. Practice walking back and forth, in straight lines, with a purpose, making 180 degree u-turns away from your dog. Remember to press the button (pressure on) as you turn and release the button (pressure off) as your dog follows through. This may be a very short time pressing the button, and you may want to use momentary here. Any time your dog is in front of you, or distracted, turn away from your dog. Remember to use your e-collar to communicate with your dog.

You will want to turn the other direction, toward your dog, as well. As you are walking in a straight line with your dog, turn at a 90 degree angle toward your dog, and keep walking straight. Turn toward your dog when your dog is pushy or not paying attention to you. Remember to press the button (pressure on) as you turn and release the button (pressure off) as your dog follows through.

When you are comfortable, change your pace and speed. Work your dog on the 15' long leash, holding just the end of it so your dog has the feel of leash-less freedom.

Your dog should follow due to their choices, not because of a tight leash.

Phase 3. When your dog is doing well and does not need leash guidance, drop the long leash and repeat, in a fenced area. Be ready to step on the leash if needed.

Phase 4. When your dog is doing well and you do not need to step on the leash, take your dog off-leash and repeat, in a fenced area.

Tell your dog "Let's go" and start walking. If your dog is out of place,

You say:

--> "Good"

You do:

Press button ------------------------------> Release button

Your dog does:

Wanders ------(Guide dog into position)----> Walks at your side

If your dog is at your side or slightly behind you, "Good"

Phase 5. Bonus - **Focused Heel**

If your dog is distracted by other dogs, people, squirrels, bicycles, or something else while on a walk with you, teach your dog a focused heel.

A focused heel is where your dog looks ahead, or at you, while walking together. If your dog looks away from you, stim. If your dog looks at you or straight ahead, tell your dog "Good" and do not stim. What is appropriate? A glance away is okay, but rubber necking after a neighbor dog is not okay. Where we walk, we have some dogs who are tethered out and behind fences, barking at us and our dogs. We use this as a training opportunity. So even if dogs are barking like maniacs, we expect our dogs to have self control.

Place

We love the Place command, and you will love the benefits that come when you teach your dog to go to a specific place and stay there. It does not matter what your dog does on Place, within reason. Your dog can stand, sit, lay down, stretch out, or curl

into a ball, as long as your dog stays on place. Imagine the possibilities... during dinner, family game night, entertaining visitors, cleaning the house, and more, you will not need to crate your dog. Your dog will not jump on people, your dog will not steal food, your dog will not eat the game pieces. Place teaches self-control and calmness. As awesome as Place is, those are only about 10% of the benefits of Place, 90% of the benefit is the state of mind shift for your dog.

The Place command gives your dog an opportunity to relax. It teaches your dog the limits to their area of concern. It can be meditation for stressed dogs. By working with different objects, you can find your dog's point of resistance, where your dog is uncomfortable, and work your dog through it. When you help your dog past that "Oh heck, no," point, your dog's confidence and trust in you will grow. You have also erased a small part of your dog's stubbornness, including getting into their kennel or into your vehicle.

We use raised place boards to teach this. Because it is raised, the rules are very clear to your dog. You can use a dog bed, towel, yoga mat, or door mat. However, it will be easier with a place board.

Phase 1. Walk your dog over the place board a few times on a shorter leash, so your dog feels the place board under foot and is comfortable walking over it. Some dogs are nervous about setting foot on the place board. For them, we flip the place board upside down, so it isn't as scary. After a few walk overs, flip it right side up and see how your dog does.

Phase 2. Walk your dog onto the place board, pausing when your dog is fully on the place board. Have your dog Sit on the place board. **Release** your dog with "Let's go," and walk away together.

Phase 3. Walk your dog toward the place board, tell your dog "Place," before your dog steps onto the place board. After you give your dog the command, press and hold the stim button as you guide your dog onto the place board, with the leash if needed. When all four paws are on place, stop the stim and praise with a happy "Good!" Release your dog with "Let's go," and walk away together.

Phase 4. Approach the place board and stop. Have your dog Sit. Tell your dog "Place," and hold the stim button. Guide your dog onto the place board, as needed. When all four paws are on place, stop the stim and praise with a happy "Good!" Release your dog with "Let's go" and walk away together.

If your dog gets off Place before released, tell your dog "No," while you stim and use the leash to guide your dog back onto place. You can think of everything off the mat as hot lava, and Stim if your dog gets off before your release.

As you can see, the Place command is a set of clear rules for your dog - go to this object and do not cross the boundaries until released. There are only two ways to end Place, when you release your dog with "Free" or "Break," which means this is over, or give another command, such as "Let's go" or "Come."

Teach your dog that distractions are not an excuse to leave Place. When your dog begins to stay with some duration, increase the difficulty. Try stepping away, crossing in front of your dog, dropping the leash and picking it up again, patting your dog on the head, or dropping food or a toy nearby. Keep your Place training controlled, so you can quickly stim and guide your dog back to Place if your dog fails and steps off. Work at the pace your dog needs. Teach your dog that nothing outside the boundary is of concern.

Start with 30 seconds. Your dog should be able to do 5 minutes by the end of the first day. By the end of the first week, your dog should easily be able to do 30 minutes or more. Our usual Place is anywhere from 30 minutes to 3 hours long. The length of time will not be as important as the state of mind that Place will create. With practice, Place will be stronger than any crate.

You say:

"Place"--------------------------------------->"Good"

You do:

Press button ----------------------------------> Release button

Your dog does:

Dog walking ----(Guide dog into position)----> Dog on place

Sit

Sit is not just a position, but a state of mind. You want your dog relaxed and focused, not vibrating with anticipation. Most dogs know Sit before we even meet. When you layer the e-collar over what your dog knows, you add to your communication repertoire.

Start by holding your leash and transmitter in your right hand, with your left hand free. Apply gentle upward pressure on leash, so your dog can not swing away from you. Using your thumb and index finger of your left hand, glide those fingers down your dog's back, with one finger on each side of your dog's spine. When you get to your dog's hip bone, just past the ridge of the bone, gently touch that spot and wait. Tell your dog to "Sit" and press the Stim button, using low level stim. Stop Stim and release leash pressure when your dog is sitting.

Remember to release your dog with a "Let's go," and walk off. Do not tap the button when you release your dog. You do not have to add the Stay command. Stay is implied with our Sit. However, *you must release your dog every single time.* We cannot emphasize that enough.

If your dog gets up before being released, tell your dog "No," and press the Stim button. If your dog stays in a Sit, job well done!

Increase the three D's - distance, distraction, and duration - one at a time. Have your dog Sit. Start to move away from your dog, keeping an eye on your dog. If your dog moves, tell your dog "No," pick up the leash and re-sit your dog, pressing the Stim button until your dog sits.

You say:

"Sit" --->"Good"

You do:

Press button ----------------------------------> Release button

Your dog does:

Dog standing ----(Guide dog into position)----> Dog sits

Down

Trust is crucial. We do not start teaching down until we have built a relationship with the dog, and have bonded together. Wait for this to happen, do not rush or force Down.

From the Heel position, with your dog on your left side and the leash loop in your right hand, drop the leash from your left hand. "U-loop" the leash under your left foot, so the leash runs from your right hand, under your left foot, and is attached to your dog's secondary collar. Hold the leash and transmitter in your right hand. Tell your dog "Down" and press the Stim button, using low level stim, and gentle leash pressure. When your dog is down, stop the Stim and mark the moment with "Good."

Remember to release your dog with a "Let's go," and walk off. Do not tap the button when you release your dog. You do not have to add the Stay command. Stay is implied with our Down. However, *you must release your dog every single time*. We cannot emphasize that enough.

If your dog gets up before being released, tell your dog "No," and press the Stim button, guiding with the leash under your foot if needed. If your dog stays in a Down, job well done!

Increase the three D's - distance, distraction, and duration - one at a time. Have your dog Down. Start to move away from your dog, keeping an eye on your dog. If your dog moves, tell your dog "No," pick up the leash and re-down your dog, pressing the Stim button until your dog downs.

You say:

"Down" ---------------------------------------> "Good"

You do:

Press button ----------------------------------> Release button

Your dog does:

Dog standing/sitting --(Guide dog into position)--> Dog downs

Distance, Distraction, Duration

There are three D's in dog training. Distance. Distraction. Duration. When your dog successfully performs the behavior that you want, it is time to increase the distance or duration. Increasing them one at a time will make it easier for your dog to succeed. When your dog is performing at distance that is acceptable to you and for an amount of time that you are happy with, it is necessary to increase the distraction level.

As you are working with your dog, keep in mind your dog's individual distraction list. Number 1 is the easiest for your dog, this could be training in your home. Number 2 is a little harder, such as training in your backyard. Number 3 is a even harder, such as training in your front yard. It goes on from there, and can go to as high of a distraction as you can imagine. This list is different for every dog, but keep the list about 10 steps long to help you see the progress that you are making with your dog's training. Start at the bottom of the list and go up in steps, making sure your dog has multiple successes on each level. Lower the distance and duration every time you move to a more distracting step on your list. Then build them up to where they were at the previous level of distraction. Have fun working with your dog to overcome all distractions but do not be disappointed if you have to regress a step or two, because it is part of learning.

Sometimes you have to go one step forward and two steps back. This applies to dog training as well. If you are having a problem, feel free to regress in your training by lowering one of the Ds. When you encourage your dog to do more, you will use regression and take a step back to an easier step as your dog needs it.

My dog's distraction list:

10.

9.

8.

7.

6.

5.

4.

3.

2.

1.

7. PROBLEM BEHAVIORS

After your dog has been introduced to Freedom, Remote Collar Training, and both of you are comfortable with it, it is time to address any remaining problem behaviors.

How do I stop my dog <u>jumping</u> on people?

As your dog is jumping up on a person, or getting ready to jump up, interrupt with Stim at a level to get your dog to quickly stop that behavior. By catching your dog when your dog is getting ready to jump up, you will interrupt that behavior and stop it from happening.

Set up training scenarios so you are ready when the situation arises.

How do I stop my dog from going <u>crazy at the door</u>?

Have a leash on your dog, attached to the secondary collar. When someone knocks on the door or rings the doorbell, call your dog to Come to you, while you Stim and guide with gentle leash pressure as needed. Set up training scenarios so you are ready when the situation arises. Also read the question and answer for "How do I stop my dog from barking?"

You can also teach your dog to Place when someone comes to your door. The Place can be beside your door, so you can concentrate on your dog as well as your visitor.

How do I stop my dog <u>pulling</u> or <u>lunging</u> on walks?

Use a regular flat leash, not a retractable leash, attached to your dog's secondary collar, not to the e-collar.

The first step is Stim Turn and Walk Away (*The Warfel Way*) with your leashed dog to break your dog's focus. Remember to bring your dog's attention back to you to stop problem behaviors.

The next step is Stim in Front. Your dog should walk at your side and at your pace. When you require your dog to walk beside you, you provide rules and a boundary for your dog. If your dog is walking in front of you, Stim. Consistency is key, your dog's front legs and shoulders should line up with your hip. If your dog starts creeping forward, Stim until you catch up to your dog. Most dogs will pause for a moment, giving you time to catch up, or they will come back to you. The quicker you are with Stim in Front, the faster your dog will learn where they should be.

Dog walking in front --------------------> Dog at your side

Press button -------------------------------> Release button

How do I stop my dog's <u>aggression</u> or <u>reactivity</u>?

Read the answer for "How do I stop my dog pulling or lunging on walks?" Follow that protocol, but Stim Turn and Walk Away (*The Warfel Way*) when your dog first notices the trigger. Do not wait for your dog to lose their mind at the trigger, or you will need to use a much higher level of Stim. Remember, the level has to be just right for that situation.

The Warfel Way - Stim Turn and Walk Away

Press the Stim button, turn your body 180 degrees, and briskly walk away with your leashed dog in that opposite direction. Walk at least 20 feet, or until your dog makes the commitment to walk with you and ignores the trigger. As soon as your dog engages with you, and ignores the trigger, stop pressing the Stim button, but continue walking at least 10 more feet. Turn and walk towards the trigger again, repeating Stim Turn and Walk Away as needed, adjusting your level so it is just right for your dog. Remember when you are setting this up as a training situation to have room behind you to walk away.

How do I stop my dog from <u>biting the leash</u>?

In the beginning, we may ignore the leash biting. Many times that behavior will just go away. If it does not, Stim when your dog starts to mouth the leash, at a level to get your dog to quickly stop that behavior. Make sure you are walking with a purpose, with your dog walking at your side and at your pace. Vibrate may work well for this behavior.

How do I stop my dog from <u>chewing,</u> <u>counter surfing,</u> <u>stealing food?</u>

You have three options with your dog. Your dog is crated. Your dog is tethered to you with a leash attached to the secondary collar. Your dog is directly supervised with e-collar on, which includes walks and play time.

When your dog first starts to do one of these undesirable behaviors, interrupt with Stim at a level to get your dog to quickly stop that behavior. Vibrate may work well for this behavior.

You do not have to say anything, because you will not always be there and you *never* want your dog to chew inappropriate objects, or swipe your food. Set up training scenarios so you are ready to correct when needed.

How do I teach my dog to <u>leave</u> objects alone?

When your dog shows an interest in the forbidden object, Stim until your dog ignores or drops the object. Stim at a level to get your dog to quickly leave that object alone. Set up training scenarios so you are ready to correct when needed.

How do I stop my dog from <u>running off</u>?

Read the step-by-step instructions under Freedom Training for Come. Remember to use a long leash so you can step on it, guiding your dog as needed, and practice multiple times each day. Do not take your dog off leash until you do not need to step on the long leash while working your dog in a safe, fenced area.

How do I stop my dog from <u>digging</u>?

Every time your dog goes outside alone, keep watch on your dog from a window, so your dog does not know that you are there. Some dogs love the act of digging, other dogs dig because they are bored. When you see your dog start to dig, Stim at a level to get your dog to quickly leave that area alone.

How do I stop my dog from <u>barking?</u>

When your dog starts barking, Stim at a level to stop your dog from barking. Be consistent. You can do this when your dog is inside with you, your dog is inside when you are outside, or when your dog is crated. Vibrate may work well for this behavior.

You can also use an electronic bark collar, which will automatically stim whenever your dog barks, whether or you are home or not. We commonly use the electronic bark collars when the board and train dogs are crated, and use the remote training collars when we are training them.

How do I stop my dog from <u>chasing</u> my cat, horse, or other pets?

Keep the long leash on your dog, and remember *The Warfel Way* (Stim Turn and Walk Away) with your leashed dog to break your dog's focus. Remember to bring your dog's attention back to you to stop problem behaviors. Stim at a level to get your dog to quickly leave that alone.

You can also **Stim for intention.** Do not wait for your dog to chase the cat around the house, instead Stim when your dog locks eyes on the cat. You want to use a level to get your dog to quickly leave your cat alone.

Depending on the behaviors, we can do **aversion training.** This is what happens when you snake proof your dog. You can also use it to cat proof, horse proof, or fence proof your dog.

But my dog is still naughty!

Make sure you and your dog are taking at least two 15-minute structured walks each day, minimum. These are training walks, with your dog walking at your side and at your pace. No matter how large your house is, or how large your yard is, you and your dog need this time together as a team, outside, and out of the yard.

You can supplement your walks with treadmill training, swimming, playtime, daycare, or a dog walker, but *you must exercise your dog,* with structure, for this minimum amount of time.

Disclaimer

This book is a supplement to our Freedom method of training at Dream Dogz Behavior Center. If you are using this book without the guidance of a professional dog trainer, skilled with low level remote collar training, your results may vary.

Index

About the Authors

Victoria Warfel

Head Trainer/Behavior Specialist

IACP-CDT/CDTA/PDTI, CTDI, CGC

Vicki is the head trainer at Dream Dogz. She has been training in the Gainesville area since she moved here in 2005 with her family and her self-trained service dog, Boo. Vicki started as a food-based trainer, but realized the limitations and kept searching for a better way. After studying and combining many styles of training, she has developed her own unique training style. Vicki quickly became the areas go-to trainer and eagerly takes on the hardest behavior issues.

She opened Dream Dogz Training & Behavior Center in 2011. Before then, she was one of the trainers at Dogwood Park and trained in the city parks.

Victoria is:

- Certified Dog Trainer (IACP-CDT).

- Certified Dog Trainer-Advanced (CDTA).

- Professional Dog Training Instructor (PDTI).

- Professional Member of the International Association of Canine Professionals (IACP).

- Professional Member of the Association of Professional Dog Trainers (APDT).

- Perception Modification I Certified in the Syn Alia Training System.

- AKC-Approved Canine Good Citizen Evaluator, Community Canine Evaluator, Urban Canine Good Citizen, S.T.A.R. Puppy Instructor & Evaluator, thru the American Kennel Club.

- the first Certified Trick Dog Instructor (CTDI) in the southeastern United States. She has earned the Trainer of the Year award!

- Therapy Dog Evaluator for Therapy Pets Unlimited, Inc.

- Founder of the Freedom, Remote Collar Training Method.

- Canine First Aid/CPR Certified thru American Red Cross.

- Volunteer with Karl's Kids Program – Alachua County Project Coordinator.

- Member of the Demand Media's Talent & Expert network, approved for on-camera projects. She is a recognized dog training expert, and so far, has been featured in two dog training video series (with 26 videos).

- Holds a bachelor's degree from the University of Wisconsin.

Richard Warfel

Head Trainer/Behavior Specialist

CTDI, CGC

Rich was in the design engineering field, and decided to leave that career path in order to take our family business to the next level. Rich enjoys spending every day training dogs and working in the sunshine. His calm, patient demeanor has quickly made him a favorite with the dogs and their owners. Rich is currently working towards his IACP Certified Dog Trainer certification.

Richard is:

- Associate Member of the International Association of Canine Professionals (IACP).

- AKC-Approved Canine Good Citizen Evaluator, Community Canine Evaluator, Urban Canine Good Citizen, S.T.A.R. Puppy Instructor & Evaluator, thru the American Kennel Club.

- Certified Trick Dog Instructor (CTDI).

- Therapy Dog Evaluator for Therapy Pets Unlimited, Inc.

- Founder of the Freedom, Remote Collar Training Method.

- Canine First Aid/CPR Certified thru American Red Cross.

Victoria & Richard are proud members of the International Association of Canine Professionals and strongly encourage you to support them.

www.canineprofessionals.com

Made in the USA
San Bernardino, CA
19 October 2017